Terrorist Watch List Screening and Brady Background Checks for Firearms

William J. Krouse
Specialist in Domestic Security and Crime Policy

February 1, 2012

Congressional Research Service
7-5700
www.crs.gov
R42336

CRS Report for Congress
Prepared for Members and Committees of Congress

Summary

The November 2009 shooting at Fort Hood, TX, renewed interest in terrorist watchlist screening and Brady background checks for firearms through the National Instant Criminal Background Check System (NICS). Pursuant to the Brady Handgun Violence Prevention Act (P.L. 103-159), in November 1998 the Federal Bureau of Investigation (FBI) activated NICS for the purposes of determining an individual's firearms transfer and possession eligibility whenever a private person seeks to acquire a firearm from a federally licensed gun dealer. Prior to February 2004, however, the FBI did not conduct terrorist watchlist queries as part of the Brady background checks because being a known or suspected terrorist was not a disqualifying factor for firearms transfer and possession eligibility; nor is it today under current law.

Following the September 11, 2001, terrorist attacks, the U.S. government reevaluated its terrorist screening procedures. As part of this process, the Department of Justice (DOJ) and FBI modified the Brady background check procedures and recalibrated NICS to query an additional file in the National Crime Information Center (NCIC) that included terrorist watchlist records. Since February 2004, information related to the subjects of NICS-generated terrorist watchlist hits have been passed on to the FBI Counterterrorism Division and special agents in the field, who are usually members of Joint Terrorism Task Forces (JTTFs). These FBI agents, in turn, verify the match between the individual and the watchlist record, and they check for information that would prohibit that individual, the prospective transferee, licensee, or permittee, from possessing firearms or explosives (e.g., illegal immigration or fugitive status).

While the modified NICS procedures initially generated little public opposition, those procedures called three possible issues into question. One, should terrorist watchlist checks be incorporated statutorily into the firearms- and explosives-related background check processes? Two, given certain statutory prohibitions related to prohibiting a firearms registry, should approved firearm transfer records be maintained on a temporary basis to determine whether persons of interest in counterterrorism investigations have obtained firearms? Three, should the Attorney General be granted authority to deny a firearms transfer based solely on a terrorist watchlist match? Since the 109th Congress, several related legislative proposals have been introduced. Several of those bills would have addressed the retention of firearms-related transfer records. Another proposal would have prohibited persons watch-listed as terrorists for aviation security purposes on the "No Fly" list from firearms transfer or possession eligibility.

In the 110th Congress, Senator Frank Lautenberg and Representative Peter King introduced a bill based on a legislative proposal developed by DOJ that would have authorized the Attorney General to deny the transfer of firearms or the issuance of firearms (and explosives) licenses/permits to "dangerous terrorists" (S. 1237/H.R. 2074). They reintroduced this proposal in the 111th Congress and supporters dubbed it the "Terror Gap" proposal (S. 1317/H.R. 2159). It was reintroduced once again in the 112th Congress (S. 34 /H.R. 1506). The Terror Gap proposal raises several potential issues for Congress. One, should the Attorney General notify watch-listed individuals who have been deemed to be "dangerous terrorists" for the purposes of gun control? Two, what form of redress and/or remedy would be provided to individuals wrongfully denied a firearm transfer because they were misidentified, or improperly watch-listed, and then deemed to be a "dangerous terrorist"? Three, if enacted, would such a law draw unwanted attention to related terrorist screening procedures, possibly undermining the effectiveness of these procedures by making terrorists and other adversaries aware of them, and possibly setting a judicial review precedent for other terrorist watchlist screening processes?

Contents

Introduction 1
Post-9/11 Reforms and Modified NICS Procedures 3
    Brady Background Checks and NICS Procedures 4
    HSPD-6 and Terrorist Watchlists 6
    DOJ-FBI Modified NICS Procedures (February 2004) 10
    GAO Report Recommendations (January 2005) 12
    Possible Issues Raised by the Modified NICS Procedures 12
    DOJ Draft Proposal (April 2007) 14
    GAO Follow-Up Report (May 2009) 15
Terror Gap Legislation 16
    HSGAC Hearing on the Fort Hood Shooting 16
    Denying Firearms and Explosives to Dangerous Terrorists Act of 2011 (S. 34 and
        H.R. 1506) 18
        Firearms Eligibility and Dangerous Terrorist Determination 19
        Notification of a Dangerous Terrorist Determination 20
        Tenth Class of Prohibited Persons Under 18 U.S.C. §922(g) 20
        Remedies for Erroneous Firearms Denials 21
        Denial and Revocation of Firearms and Explosives Licenses 22
        Attorney General Implementing Guidelines 22
Possible Policy Issues Raised by the Terror Gap Proposal 22
    Would the Proposed Non-notification Authority Be Feasible? 23
    Would Adequate Opportunity for Redress and Remedy Be Provided? 23
    Would a Precedent Be Set for Other Screening Processes? 23

Appendixes

Appendix. Acronyms and Abbreviations 24

Contacts

Author Contact Information 25
Acknowledgments 25

Introduction

Following the September 11, 2001, terrorist attacks (9/11 attacks), the George W. Bush Administration took measures to consolidate and expand the use of terrorist watchlists maintained by the federal government. As part of this process, the Department of Justice (DOJ) directed the Federal Bureau of Investigation (FBI) to modify their firearms- and explosives-related background check procedures to screen prospective firearms buyers and state-issued permit applicants (Brady background checks), as well as explosives license and permit applicants, against terrorist watchlist records.[1] Those modified procedures became effective in February 2004. In addition, under the modified procedures FBI counterterrorism agents found it useful and arguably prudent to maintain and share information about terrorist watchlist-related matches for approved firearms transfer records. However, a provision of federal firearms law requires that all approved firearms transfer records held by the National Instant Criminal Background Checks System (NICS), including those related to terrorist watchlist hits, be destroyed within 24 hours.

While the Attorney General has no specific statutory authority to screen those buyers and applicants against the terrorist watchlist records nor maintain records on approved firearms transfers for longer than 24 hours, the modified background check procedures initially generated little public outcry from opponents of greater federal gun control. At the same time, several Members of Congress raised public safety concerns about the possibility that terrorists might exploit the general availability of firearms in the United States. They tasked the Government Accountability Office (GAO) with evaluating the modified Brady background check procedures for firearms and, later, background check procedures for explosives. Since then, GAO has reported on several occasions that subjects of positive terrorist watchlist hits were transferred firearms and, less frequently, explosives.[2] Over nearly seven years (2004-2010), 1,453 federal firearms-related background checks resulted in terrorist watchlist matches; 1,321 (90.9%) were allowed to proceed.[3] Those transfers were allowed to proceed because being on a terrorist

---

[1] The Brady background check procedures were established pursuant to the Brady Handgun Violence Prevention Act (known as the "Brady Act"; P.L. 103-159; November 30 1993; 107 Stat. 1536). The permanent provisions of the Brady Act became effective on November 30, 1998, with the activation of the National Instant Criminal Background Check System. The Brady Act amended the Gun Control Act of 1968 (GCA; P.L. 90-618; October 22, 1968; 82 Stat. 1213). The GCA is codified, as amended, at 18 U.S.C. §§921 *et seq*. For further information, see CRS Report RL32842, *Gun Control Legislation*, by William J. Krouse.

As part of the Homeland Security Act of 2002 (P.L. 107-296; November 25, 2002; 116 Stat. 2135), Congress amended federal explosives statutes with the Safe Explosives Act (SEA; 116 Stat. 2280). SEA added additional categories of prohibited persons, extended the licensing requirement to persons who transfer or ship explosives in intrastate commerce, and requires employees who handle explosives to undergo background checks. The federal statutes regulating explosives commerce in the United States were enacted under Title XI of the Organized Crime Control Act of 1970 (P.L. 91-452; 84 Stat. 952 (1970)). These statutes are codified, as amended, at 18 U.S.C. §§841 *et seq*.

Pursuant to SEA, in February 2003 the FBI began conducting Brady background checks on all applicants for a federal explosives license or permit for the ATF.

[2] U.S. Government Accountability Office, *Gun Control and Terrorism: FBI Could Better Manage Firearm-Related Background Checks Involving Terrorist Watch List Records*, GAO-05-127, January 2005; *Firearm and Explosives Background Checks Involving Terrorist Watch List Records*, GAO-09-125R, for the Honorable John Conyers, Jr., the Honorable Robert C. Scott, and the Honorable Frank R. Lautenberg, May 21, 2009; and *Terrorist Watchlist Screening: FBI Has Enhanced Its Use of Information from Firearm and Explosives Background Checks to Support Counterterrorism Efforts*, GAO-10-703T, May 5, 2010.

[3] U.S. Government Accountability Office, *Update on Firearm and Explosives Background Checks Involving Terrorist Watch List Records*, for the Honorable Frank R. Lautenberg, United States Senate, April 27, 2011, p. 2.

watchlist is not, in and of itself, a disqualifying factor under either federal firearms or explosives law.

GAO's confirmation that firearms have been transferred from federally licensed gun dealers to individuals watch-listed as known or suspected terrorists has lent impetus to a legislative proposal that was originally developed by DOJ, under Attorney General Alberto Gonzales, and submitted to Congress in April 2007. This proposal would give the Attorney General discretionary authority to deny firearms or explosives transfers to any watch-listed individuals if he deemed them to be "dangerous terrorists." In the 110th Congress, Senator Frank Lautenberg and Representative Peter King introduced this proposal as the Denying Firearms and Explosives to Dangerous Terrorists Act of 2007 (S. 1237/H.R. 2074). Supporters later dubbed this bill the "Terror Gap" proposal.

In the 111th Congress, the November 2009 Fort Hood shooting renewed interest in this proposal, which Senator Lautenberg and Representative King had previously reintroduced (S. 1317/H.R. 2159). In May 2010, the Senate Homeland Security and Governmental Affairs Committee (HSGAC) held a hearing on "terrorists and guns" and debated the need to pass legislation like the Terror Gap proposal. While no further action was taken on the bill, Senator Lautenberg and Representative King reintroduced the Terror Gap proposal (S. 34/H.R. 1506) in the 112th Congress. This report examines potential policy issues that could arise under the Terror Gap proposal. Possible issues could include the following:

- Should U.S. persons—citizens and legal permanent residents—be notified when the Attorney General makes a "dangerous terrorist" determination about them for the purposes of gun control following a terrorist watchlist match?

- What form of redress and remedy would be provided for misidentifications, improper watch-listing, and wrongful denial? If enacted, moreover, would these redress and remedy provisions serve as a precedent for other terrorist screening procedures for which Congress has not provided similar avenues of relief?

- Would the Terror Gap proposal draw unwanted public attention to terrorist watchlists and related screening procedures, possibly undermining the effectiveness of those measures by making terrorists and other adversaries aware of them, and possibly setting a judicial review precedent for other terrorist watchlist screening processes?

As noted above, the Terror Gap proposal would grant the Attorney General the authority to deny firearms transfers and state-issued firearms permits,[4] as well as federal licenses to deal in firearms, to watchlisted persons if he deemed them to be "dangerous terrorists." The proposal would also grant the Attorney General similar authority to deny federal licenses to deal in explosives or federal permits to handle explosives. However, the gravity of a denial of a federal license to deal in either firearms or explosives, or a federal permit to handle explosives—which is arguably the denial of a privilege as opposed to a constitutionally enumerated right—would not

---

[4] While federal law does not require a private person to acquire a firearms license or permit for the purposes of firearms possession or transfer (purchase) eligibility, some states require an individual to acquire such documentation for that purpose. For example, Hawaii, Illinois, Massachusetts, New Jersey, and the District of Columbia require either a license or permit for eligibility for any firearms (handguns or long guns). By comparison, California, Connecticut, Iowa, Maryland, Michigan, Minnesota, Nebraska, North Carolina, Pennsylvania, and Rhode Island require either a license or permit for eligibility for handguns only. In these states, Brady background checks are performed prior to license or permit issuance.

be as compelling as the denial of a firearms transfer or state-issued permit to an individual.[5] Hence, the principal focus of this report is on the potential policy issues that could be generated by the denial of a firearms transfer or a state-issued permit to an individual under the Terror Gap proposal. Although the due process issues raised by the Terror Gap proposal are not addressed in this report, the arguably parallel policy issues are examined in detail. To further this examination, this report provides (1) an overview of the post-9/11 reforms that led to the incorporation of terrorist watchlist checks into the Brady background check process, (2) an analysis of key provisions of the Terror Gap proposal, and (3) a summation of possible issues for Congress.

Post-9/11 Reforms and Modified NICS Procedures

Under the Brady Handgun Violence Prevention Act (Brady Act),[6] Congress required the Attorney General to establish a computerized system to facilitate background checks on individuals seeking to acquire a firearm from federally licensed gun dealers. Under the permanent provisions of the Brady Act, the FBI activated the NICS on November 30, 1998.[7] Initially, the FBI did not conduct terrorist watchlist queries through NICS as part of Brady background checks for firearms because being a known or suspected terrorist was not, and is not, a legally disqualifying factor for firearms possession eligibility under federal law. Conducting terrorist watchlist checks as part of Brady background checks for firearms raises three possible issues for Congress:

- Should terrorist watchlist checks be incorporated statutorily into the Brady background check processes?

- Given certain statutory restrictions prohibiting a permanent or temporary registry of firearms or firearms owners, should approved firearm transfer records be maintained on a temporary basis to determine whether persons of interest in counterterrorism investigations had or have obtained firearms?[8]

- Should the Attorney General be granted authority to deny a firearms transfer based solely on a terrorist watchlist match?

To explore these issues in greater depth, the modified Brady background check procedures, which were adopted in February 2004, are discussed below.

---

[5] The possible constitutional due process interests at stake under the Terror Gap proposal are arguably elevated by recent Supreme Court decisions. For further information, see CRS Report R41750, *The Second Amendment: An Overview of District of Columbia v. Heller and McDonald v. City of Chicago*, by Vivian S. Chu.

[6] P.L. 103-159; November 30, 1993, 107 Stat. 1536.

[7] Under the interim provisions of the Brady Act (November 30, 1993, through November 30, 1998), federally licensed gun dealers were required to contact state and local chief law enforcement officers to determine the eligibility of prospective customers to be transferred a handgun.

[8] As described below, the Brady Act includes a provision that prohibits using NICS-generated records to establish a registry of firearms, firearms owners, or firearms transfers and dispositions. In January 2005, the Government Accountability Office (GAO) recommended that the Attorney General clarify what information generated by the NICS background check process could be shared with counterterrorism officials. However, whether the Attorney General acted on this recommendation is not part of the public record. In the absence of any clarification made by the Attorney General, the maintenance of NICS-generated records related to approved firearms transfers for any purposes not expressly authorized under the Brady Act could be viewed as being at cross purposes with that act.

Brady Background Checks and NICS Procedures

Prior to the 1993 Brady Act, five states had established computerized, name-based criminal history record background check systems for firearms.[9] However, the federal system under the Gun Control Act was largely paper-based. The Brady Act built upon this paper-based system, which essentially entailed the following procedures. When a private person (non-licensee) seeks to acquire a firearm (long gun or handgun) from a federally licensed gun dealer, he and the gun dealer are required to fill out ATF Form 4473. The gun dealer is also required to verify the purchaser's name, address, date of birth, and other information by examining a state-issued piece of identification, most often a driver's license. As the prospective transferee, the private person attests on ATF Form 4473, under penalty of perjury, that he is not a prohibited person.

Under current law, there are 10 classes of prohibited persons. Nine of those classes are prohibited from shipping, transporting, receiving, or possessing firearms or ammunition. They include

- persons convicted in any court of a crime punishable by imprisonment for a term exceeding one year;
- fugitives from justice;
- unlawful users or addicts of any controlled substance as defined in Section 102 of the Controlled Substances Act (21 U.S.C. §802));
- persons adjudicated as "mental defectives" or committed to mental institutions;
- illegal/unauthorized immigrants and most nonimmigrant aliens (with some exceptions in the latter case);
- persons dishonorably discharged from the U.S. Armed Forces;
- persons who have renounced their U.S. citizenship;
- persons under court-order restraints related to harassing, stalking, or threatening an intimate partner or child of such intimate partner; and
- persons convicted of misdemeanor domestic violence.[10]

In addition, a 10th class of persons is prohibited from shipping, transporting, or receiving firearms or ammunition. It includes

- persons under indictment in any court of a crime punishable by imprisonment for a term exceeding one year.[11]

As part of a Brady background check process, a federally licensed gun dealer is required to submit a prospective firearms transferee's name, sex, race, date of birth, and state of residence to the FBI through NICS. Social security numbers and other numeric identifiers are optional, but the submission of these data is likely to increase the timeliness of the background check (and reduce misidentifications).[12] The transferee's information is crosschecked against three computerized

---

[9] Those states were Delaware, Florida, Illinois, Rhode Island, and Virginia.

[10] 18 U.S.C. §922(g).

[11] 18 U.S.C. §922(n).

[12] NICS is designed to turn firearms-related background checks around within minutes, but as described below, if necessary a firearms transfer can be delayed under current law for up to three business days. Such delays are usually (continued...)

databases/systems to determine firearms transfer/possession eligibility. Those systems include the Interstate Identification Index (III), National Crime Information Center (NCIC), and NICS index.[13] If the transferee indicates that he is a non-U.S. citizen, his information is also checked against the immigration and naturalization databases maintained by the Department of Homeland Security (DHS), Immigration and Customs Enforcement (ICE).[14]

The FBI handles background checks entirely for most states, while other states serve as full or partial points of contact (POCs) for firearms background check purposes. In POC states, federally licensed gun dealers contact a state agency, and the state agency contacts the FBI for Brady background checks.[15] Under no circumstances is a federally licensed gun dealer informed about the prohibiting factor upon which a denial is based.[16] A denied person is also not informed initially about the reason for his denial. However, a denied person may challenge the accuracy of the underlying record(s) upon which his denial is based.[17] He would initiate this process by requesting (usually in writing) the reason for the denial from the agency that conducted the NICS check (the FBI or POC). The denying agency has five business days to respond to the request. Upon receipt of the reason and underlying record for the denial, the denied person may challenge the accuracy of that record. If the record is found to be inaccurate, the denying agency is legally obligated to correct that record.

As with other screening systems, particularly those that are name-based, false positives occur as a result of Brady background checks. Although the frequency of these misidentifications has not been reported, the FBI has taken steps to mitigate false positives. In July 2004, DOJ issued a

---

(...continued)
the result of partial or incomplete criminal history records that require the FBI to contact state and local authorities to finalize a determination about the transferee's firearms possession eligibility.

[13] The III, or "Triple I," is a computerized criminal history index pointer system that the FBI maintains so that records on persons arrested and convicted of felonies and serious misdemeanors at either the federal or state level can be shared nationally. The NCIC is a database of documented criminal justice information that is made available to law enforcement and authorized agencies, with the goal of assisting law enforcement in apprehending fugitives, finding missing persons, locating stolen property, and further protecting law enforcement personnel and the public. The NICS index contains disqualifying records not found in either the III or NCIC on all the classes of prohibited persons enumerated in the GCA.

[14] Those databases include the Central Index System (CIS); Computer Linked Application Information Management System (CLAIMS); Deportable Alien Control System (DACS); National Automated Immigration Lookout System (NAIL II); Nonimmigrant Information System (NIIS); Student and Exchange Visitor Information System (SEVIS); Redesigned Naturalization Casework System (RNACS); Refugee, Asylum, and Parole System (RAPS); Enforcement Case Tracking System (ENFORCE); and the Treasury Enforcement Communications System (TECS).

[15] In 13 states, state agencies serve as full POCs and conduct Brady background checks for both long gun and handgun transfers. In four states, state agencies serve as partial POCs for handgun permits; in four other states, state agencies serve as partial POCs for handgun transfers only. In these eight partial POC states, checks for long gun transfers are conducted entirely through the FBI. In the 30 non-POC states, the District of Columbia, and five territories (American Samoa, Guam, Northern Mariana Islands, Puerto Rico, and the Virgin Islands), federally licensed gun dealers contact the FBI directly to conduct background checks through NICS for both handgun and long gun transfers. For state agencies (POCs), background checks may not be as expeditious, but they may be more thorough because state agencies may have greater access to databases and records that are not available through NICS. According to the Government Accountability Office (GAO), this is particularly true for domestic violence misdemeanor offenses and protective orders. For further information, see GAO, *Gun Control: Opportunities to Close Loopholes in the National Instant Criminal Background Check System*, GAO-02-720, July 2002, p. 27.

[16] Statement of Daniel D. Roberts, Assistant Director, Criminal Justice Information Services, Federal Bureau of Investigation, *Terrorists and Guns: The Nature of the Threat and Proposed Reforms: Hearing Before the S. Comm. on Homeland Sec. and Gov't Affairs*, 111th Cong., May 5, 2010.

[17] Correction of Erroneous System Information, 28 C.F.R. §25.10.

regulation that established the NICS Voluntary Appeal File (VAF), which is part of the NICS Index (described above).[18] DOJ was prompted to establish the VAF to minimize the inconvenience incurred by some prospective firearms transferees (purchasers) who have names or birth dates similar to those of prohibited persons. These persons agree to authorize the FBI to maintain personally identifying information about them in the VAF as a means to avoid future misidentifications and delayed transfers. Current law requires that NICS records on approved firearms transfers, particularly information personally identifying the transferee, be destroyed within 24 hours.[19]

There is also a provision of federal law that allows the Attorney General to consider petitions from a prohibited person for "relief from disabilities" and have his firearms transfer and possession eligibility restored.[20] Since FY1993, however, a rider on the ATF annual appropriations for salaries and expenses has prohibited the expenditure of any funding provided under that account on processing such petitions.[21] While a prohibited person could petition the Attorney General, bypassing ATF, such an alternative has never been successfully tested. As a result, the only way a person can reacquire his lost firearms eligibility is to have his civil rights restored or disqualifying criminal record(s) expunged or set aside, or to be pardoned for his crime.

HSPD-6 and Terrorist Watchlists

In September 2003, the U.S. government moved to consolidate and expand its use of watchlists to better screen for known or suspected terrorists at consular offices and international ports of entry, and to better track them if they manage to enter the United States. This effort came under Homeland Security Presidential Directive 6 (HSPD-6), which is discussed below.[22] Prior to the 9/11 attacks, terrorist watchlists were maintained by several agencies primarily to prevent international (foreign) terrorists from entering the United States.

Under HSPD-6, the Attorney General established the Terrorist Screening Center (TSC) to consolidate the U.S. government's approach to screening both international and domestic terrorists.[23] The National Counterterrorism Center (NCTC) also plays a pivotal role, because it

---

[18] Final Rule, National Instant Criminal Background Check System Regulation, 69 *Federal Register* 43892 (July 23, 2004) (codified at 28 C.F.R. §25.10(g)).

[19] For FY2009, see Section 511 of the Omnibus Appropriations Act, 2009, (P.L. 111-8, 123 Stat. 596). In the Consolidated and Further Continuing Appropriations Act, 2012 (P.L. 112-55), Congress strengthened the "futurity" language, which makes this proviso permanent law, as opposed to an annual appropriations restriction. Nevertheless, for FY2010 it was included in the Consolidated Appropriations Act, 2010 (P.L. 111-117). For FY2011, notwithstanding the "futurity" language, the provision was carried over in the Department of Defense and Full-Year Continuing Appropriations Act, 2011 (P.L. 112-10). For FY2012, the provision was also included in the Consolidated and Further Continuing Appropriations Act, 2012 (P.L. 112-55).

[20] 18 U.S.C. §925(c). See also Relief from Disabilities Under the Act, 27 C.F.R. §478.144.

[21] For FY1993, see P.L. 102-393; 106 Stat. 1732 (1992). For FY2012, see P.L. 112-55; 125 Stat. 609 (2011). The FY2012 limitation provides "that none of the funds appropriated herein shall be available to investigate or act upon applications for relief from Federal firearms disabilities under 18 U.S.C. 925(c)."

[22] Homeland Security Presidential Directive 6 (HSPD-6), *Integration and Use of Screening Information* (September 16, 2003), http://www.dhs.gov/xabout/laws/gc_1214594853475.shtm.

[23] According to the FBI, international terrorists include those persons who carry out terrorist activities *under foreign direction*. For this purpose, they may include both citizens and noncitizens; citizens are included under the rationale that they could be recruited by foreign terrorist groups. Or, noncitizens (aliens) could immigrate to the United States and naturalize (become citizens), having been unidentified terrorists before entry, or having been recruited as terrorists (continued...)

serves as the U.S. government's central and shared knowledge bank on known or suspected international terrorists and international terrorist groups. The NCTC maintains the Terrorist Identities Datamart Environment (TIDE), the U.S. government's central repository on international terrorist identities and principal source of international terrorist screening records.[24] Federal agencies within the U.S. Intelligence community (IC)[25] forward nominations to the NCTC to place persons known or suspected to be international terrorists into TIDE based on evaluations of intelligence and law enforcement information.[26] According to NCTC, if a person engages in certain types of conduct, it could warrant their entry into TIDE, and possibly a terrorist screening nomination as well. Examples of that conduct could include

- commits international terrorist activity;
- prepares or plans international terrorist activity;
- gathers information on potential targets for international terrorist activity;
- solicits funds or other things of value for international terrorist activity or a terrorist organization;
- solicits membership in an international terrorist organization;
- provides material support (e.g., safe house, transportation, communications, funds, transfer of funds or other material financial benefit, false documentation or identification, weapons, explosives, or training); or
- is a member of or represents a foreign terrorist organization.[27]

(...continued)
sometime after their entry into the United States. By comparison, domestic terrorists *are not under foreign direction* and operate entirely within the United States. According to the Administration, both sets of data (on international and domestic terrorists) include, when appropriate, information on "United States persons." The definition of "United States person" is found at 50 U.S.C. §1801(i): a citizen of the United States, an alien lawfully admitted for permanent residence (as defined in §1101(a)(2) of Title 8), an unincorporated association of which a substantial number of members are citizens of the United States or aliens lawfully admitted for permanent residence, or a corporation that is incorporated in the United States, but does not include a corporation or an association that is a foreign power, as defined in subsection (a)(1), (2), or (3) of this section.

[24] Pursuant to the Intelligence Reform and Terrorism Prevention Act of 2004 (P.L. 108-458), the NCTC (formerly, the Terrorist Threat Integration Center) was charged with serving as the primary organization in the U.S. government for analyzing and integrating all intelligence possessed or acquired by the U.S. government pertaining to terrorism or counterterrorism, excepting law enforcement information (criminal intelligence) pertaining exclusively to domestic terrorists and domestic terrorism. The NCTC was placed under the aegis of the Director of National Intelligence (DNI).

[25] The intelligence community includes the Office of the Director of National Intelligence (ODNI), Central Intelligence Agency (CIA); the National Security Agency (NSA); the Defense Intelligence Agency (DIA); the National Geospatial-Intelligence Agency (NGA); the National Reconnaissance Office (NRO); the other DOD offices that specialize in national intelligence through reconnaissance programs; the intelligence components of the Army, Navy, Air Force, and Marine Corps; the FBI; the Drug Enforcement Administration (DEA); the Department of Energy; the Coast Guard; the Bureau of Intelligence and Research (INR) at the Department of State (DOS); the Office of Intelligence and Analysis at the Department of the Treasury; and elements of the Department of Homeland Security (DHS) that are concerned with the analyses of foreign intelligence information (50 U.S.C. §401a(4)).

[26] National Counterterrorism Center, "Terrorist Identities Datamart Environment (TIDE) Fact Sheet," http://www.nctc.gov/docs/Tide_Fact_Sheet.pdf.

[27] Ibid.

As of December 2011, TIDE contained over 740,000 persons, most with multiple minor spelling variations of their names.[28] U.S. persons (including both citizens and legal permanent residents) made up less than 2% of TIDE listings.[29] The NCTC supports the U.S. government's various terrorist screening operations by providing unclassified, "For Official Use Only," international terrorist screening records to the FBI-administered TSC for inclusion in the Terrorist Screening Database (TSDB). As of May 2010, the TSDB contained information on 423,000 individuals.[30] According to the TSC, U.S. persons make up about 5% of TSDB listings.[31]

Although there is little information about the terrorist nomination processes for other IC entities, according to a May 2009 DOJ Inspector General's audit, FBI Special Agents investigating international counterterrorism cases forward watchlist nominations on international terrorists to the NCTC for inclusion in TIDE and, subsequently, that information is forwarded to the TSC for inclusion in the TSDB.[32] In addition, FBI Special Agents investigating domestic counterterrorism cases forward domestic terrorist watchlist nominations directly to the TSC for inclusion in the TSDB.[33] Hence, the TSDB is the U.S. government's consolidated watchlist of all known or suspected terrorists, whether they are of the international or domestic type.

It is noteworthy that, in the Intelligence Reform and Terrorism Prevention Act of 2004 (P.L. 108-458), Congress required the Director of National Intelligence (DNI), in consultation with the Secretary of Homeland Security, the Secretary of State, and the Attorney General, to report to Congress on the criteria for placing individuals in the TSDB, including minimum standards for reliability and accuracy of identifying information, the threat levels posed by listed persons, and the appropriate responses to be taken if those persons were encountered.[34] While it is unknown whether the DNI reported to Congress on this matter, in another report, the DHS Privacy Office underscored that those criteria could not be made public without (1) compromising intelligence and security or (2) allowing persons wishing to avoid detection to subvert those lists.[35] In October 2007, the GAO reported that the FBI and Intelligence Community were using reasonable standards for watch-listing persons who are suspected of having possible links to terrorism.[36]

The TSC shares TSDB-generated terrorist screening records with frontline screening agencies for inclusion in their computer systems. The TSC, moreover, tailors those records and shares them in accordance with the missions and legal authorities under which the screening agencies operate.[37]

---

[28] Ibid.

[29] Ibid.

[30] Federal Bureau of Investigation, Office of Congressional Affairs.

[31] Terrorist Screening Center, http://www.fbi.gov/fbi-search?cx=004748461833896749646%3Ae41lgwqry7w&cof=FORID%3A10%3BNB%3A1&ie=UTF-8&q=Terrorist+Screening+Center+Statistics&siteurl=www.fbi.gov%2F.

[32] U.S. Department of Justice, Office of the Inspector General, *Federal Bureau of Investigation's Terrorist Watchlist Nomination Practices*, Audit Report 09-25, May 2009, p. 13.

[33] Ibid.

[34] See Section 4012(c); 118 Stat. 3718 (2004).

[35] U.S. Department of Homeland Security, *DHS Privacy Office Report on Assessing the Impact of the Automatic Selectee and No Fly Lists on Privacy and Civil Liberties*, April 27, 2006, p. 9.

[36] U.S. Government Accountability Office, *Terrorist Watch List Screening, Opportunities Exist to Enhance Management Oversight, Reduce Vulnerabilities in Agency Screening Processes, and Expand the Use of the List*, GAO-08-110, October 2007, p. 19.

[37] For example, the TSC supports the terrorist screening activities of frontline screening agencies, like DHS's Transportation Security Administration (TSA) and Customs and Border Protection (CBP), as well as the Department of (continued...)

Hence, those shared terrorist screening records are subsets of the TSDB, and are often viewed by observers to be distinct terrorist watchlists despite the intent of HSPD-6. Periodically, usually coinciding with a perceived U.S. government failure to watch-list a known or suspected terrorist properly, critics of the status quo have argued that visa and passport applicants, as well as air passengers, ought to be screened against the full set of available government data on potential terrorist threats.[38]

The TSC director, in coordination with other federal agencies and national security staff, develops policies and procedures related to the criteria for including terrorist identities data in the form of terrorist screening records (or watchlist records) in the TSDB. All the data entered into the TSDB are collected by other agencies in accordance with applicable, pre-existing authorities. Although the TSC is not limited in its ability to address certain issues related to misidentifications because it has access to classified or law enforcement-sensitive information, it is restricted from divulging that information to the public. In a similar fashion, frontline screening agencies, such as the Transportation Security Administration (TSA) and U.S. Customs and Border Protection (CBP), have access to both unclassified traveler identifying information and sensitive intelligence or law enforcement information collected by other agencies. Such records would be considered security-sensitive information. Hence, it is generally the policy of the federal government neither to confirm nor deny whether any individual is on a terrorist watchlist.

While the post-9/11 terrorist screening policies have resulted in positive terrorist watchlist matches and encounters, misidentifications and erroneous watchlist entries have also been a recurring concern for Congress.[39] Initially, these problems were most frequently associated with TSA, but they also emerged as a problem for CBP.[40] DHS addressed misidentifications and

---

(...continued)

State's Bureau of Consular Affairs (CA). Similar terrorist watchlist records are also shared with the Department of Defense and selected foreign governments. In practice, a much greater percentage of TSDB-generated terrorist screening records is provided to CA for purposes of screening visa applicants than is provided to TSA for purposes of screening air passengers. As a practical matter, policymakers attempt to strike a balance between detecting threats and minimizing false positives. For further information, see CRS Report RL33645, *Terrorist Watchlist Checks and Air Passenger Prescreening*, by William J. Krouse and Bart Elias.

[38] By extension, the same argument could be made for persons undergoing firearms-related Brady background checks.

[39] The Intelligence Reform and Terrorism Prevention Act of 2004 (P.L. 108-458) required the TSA and DHS to establish appeals procedures by which persons who are identified as security threats based on records in the TSDB may appeal such determinations and have such records, if warranted, modified to alleviate such occurrences in the future. Also, provisions in the Implementing Recommendations of the 9/11 Commission Act of 2007 (P.L. 110-53) required DHS to establish an Office of Appeals and Redress to establish a timely and fair process for individuals who believe they have been delayed or prohibited from boarding a commercial aircraft because they were wrongly identified as a threat. The provisions further establish a requirement to maintain records of those passengers and individuals who have been misidentified and have corrected erroneous information. (See 49 U.S.C. §§44903, 44909, and 44926.)

In addition, in the 111th Congress, the House passed the FAST Redress Act (H.R. 559) under suspension of the rules on February 3, 2009, a bill introduced by Representative Yvette D. Clarke. This bill was similar to a proposal (H.R. 4179) passed in the 110th Congress, also introduced by Representative Clarke. Senator Amy Klobuchar introduced an identical proposal (S. 3392). The FAST Redress Act would have amended the Homeland Security Act of 2002 (P.L. 107-296) to direct the Secretary of Homeland Security to establish a timely and fair process for individuals who believe they were delayed or prohibited from boarding a commercial aircraft because they were wrongly identified as a threat when screened against any terrorist watchlist or database used by TSA or any component of DHS. It would have also authorized an Office of Appeals and Redress within DHS to implement, coordinate, and execute this process. If enacted, these bills would have arguably replicated and, thus, emphasized existing law.

[40] See, for example, Rahman v. Chertoff, 530 F. 3d 622 (7th Cir. 2008). In this suit travelers alleged that delays attributable to watchlist-related misidentifications constituted a violation of their Fourth and Fifth Amendment rights. This suit was later dismissed in district court. See Rahman v. Chertoff, No. 05-C 3761, 2010 U.S. Dist. LEXIS 31634 (continued...)

erroneous watchlist entries through its Traveler Redress and Inquiry Program (TRIP) and earlier efforts, such as, TSA's Office for Transportation Security Redress (OTSR).[41] In addition, individuals who believe they have been denied boarding or unduly scrutinized in secondary screening/inspections, because they believe they have been misidentified as a terrorist while being screened by TSA or CBP, have another avenue for relief. If they feel that the relief and/or remedy provided under TRIP was unsatisfactory, they may pursue administrative review of TRIP determinations in federal court. To date, Congress and the Administration have shown little inclination toward providing any further judicial review to persons adversely affected by terrorist watchlist screening.[42]

DOJ-FBI Modified NICS Procedures (February 2004)

In November 2003, DOJ directed the FBI to reassess its NICS procedures to include measures to screen prospective firearms transferees and permittees against terrorist watchlist records.[43] This reassessment was arguably taken in tandem with the terrorist watchlist reforms initiated under HSPD-6, as well as a February 2002 NICS transaction audit in which it was determined that prohibited aliens (noncitizens) had been improperly transferred firearms.[44]

Effective February 2004, the FBI began routinely running background checks for firearms and explosives against a terrorist watchlist that resides in NCIC because inclusion on such a list suggests that there may be an underlying factor that would bar the prospective transferee, licensee, or permittee from possessing firearms or explosives.[45] Following the 9/11 attacks, a subset of terrorist watchlist records that was included in an NCIC file designated by the FBI as

---

(...continued)
(N.D. Ill. March 31, 2010).

[41] Also, in December 2010, TSA fully implemented its Secure Flight program and the frequency of terrorist watchlist misidentifications is expected to abate. See Department of Homeland Security. *DHS Now Vetting 100 Percent Of Passengers On Flights Within Or Bound For U.S. Against Watchlists*, Press Release, November 30, 2010.

[42] Some commentators who have analyzed the larger watchlist architecture under HSPD-6 have maintained that there is an absence of a transparent, accurate, and timely redress process for persons misidentified or wrongly placed on a watchlist as a known or suspected terrorist. For example, one legal memorandum published by the Heritage Foundation posited that although terrorist watchlist screening programs offer a viable response to the problem of terrorism, such screening programs would only be acceptable if they included a robust redress process that allowed for the correction of false positives (i.e., individuals being wrongly matched or wrongly listed). It recommended both administrative review and a private right of action to appeal an adverse administrative action. Further, it recommended that judicial review of an administrative action should be de novo and that once a watch-listed individual establishes a prima facie case that his continuing presence on the watchlist is without foundation, the burden would shift to the government to prove the contrary by clear and convincing evidence, which is a more stringent than preponderance of the evidence. See Paul Rosenzweig and Jeff Jonas, *Correcting False Positives: Redress and the Watch List Conundrum*, Heritage Foundation, no. 17 (June 17, 2005), pp. 9-10. http://s3.amazonaws.com/thf_media/2005/pdf/lm17.pdf; see also Constitution Project, *Promoting Accuracy and Fairness in the Use of Government Watch Lists*, December 2006, http://www.constitutionproject.org/pdf/53.pdf.

[43] U.S. Government Accountability Office, *Gun Control and Terrorism: FBI Could Better Manage Firearm-Related Background Checks Involving Terrorist Watch List Records*, GAO-05-127, January 2005, p. 2.

[44] It is notable that unauthorized immigrants and most nonimmigrant aliens are prohibited from possessing firearms in the United States. Nonimmigrant aliens are noncitizens who have been admitted to the United States on a temporary basis, as opposed to immigrants (legal permanent residents) who have been admitted to the United States on a permanent basis.

[45] Dan Eggen, "FBI Gets More Time on Gun Buys," *Washington Post*, November 22, 2003, p. A05. See also U.S. Government Accountability Office, *Gun Control and Terrorism: FBI Could Better Manage Firearm-Related Background Checks Involving Terrorist Watch List Records*, GAO-05-127, 2005, p. 7.

the Violent Gang and Terrorist Organization File (VGTOF) was substantially expanded with TSDB-generated terrorist screening records. Later, the FBI segregated the gang- and terrorist-related records in NCIC-VGTOF, and terrorist screening records are currently downloaded into an NCIC file designated by the FBI to be the "Known or Suspected Terrorist File (KST File)."

As part of the Brady background check process, NICS typically responds to a federally licensed gun dealer, otherwise known as a federal firearms licensee (FFL), with a NICS Transaction Number (NTN) and one of three outcomes: (1) "proceed" with transfer or permit/license issuance because no prohibiting record was found; (2) "denied," indicating that a prohibiting record was found; or (3) "delayed," indicating that the system produced information suggesting that there could be a prohibiting record.[46] In the case of a possible watchlist match, NICS sends a delayed transfer (for up to three business days) response to the querying federally licensed gun dealer or state POC. During a delay, NICS staff contacts immediately the FBI Headquarters' Counterterrorism Division and FBI Special Agents in the field, and a coordinated effort is made to research possibly unknown prohibiting factors. If no prohibiting factors are uncovered within this three-day period, firearms dealers may proceed with the transaction at their discretion. However, FBI counterterrorism officials continue to work the case for up to 90 days in case disposition information is returned that permits a final determination.[47]

To assist in verifying whether a KST hit is a positive encounter (a match), NICS staff often contact the federally licensed gun dealer to gain additional information on the applicant, such as his address, driver's license number, social security number, or alien registration number (if applicable).[48] It is noteworthy, however, that GAO reported that federally licensed gun dealers are not legally obligated to provide NICS staff with this additional identifying information.[49] If NICS and TSC staff believes the KST hit is a verified, positive encounter, the TSC staff will forward this information to the FBI's Terrorist Screening Operations Unit (TSOU).[50] Next, NICS staff and the TSOU agent handling the encounter take further steps to make a final determination that the KST hit is a positive encounter.[51]

At this juncture, the FBI Counterterrorism Division and the TSOU agent determine whether the applicant is the subject of an FBI investigation.[52] If so, efforts will be made to coordinate with the appropriate Joint Terrorism Task Force (JTTF) and verify whether FBI Special Agents in the field have any disqualifying information on the applicant with which to block the transaction.[53] If the applicant is not under investigation, then the FBI will generally initiate an investigation based

---

[46] Accessing Records in the System, 28 C.F.R. §25.6.

[47] U.S. Government Accountability Office, *Gun Control and Terrorism: FBI Could Better Manage Firearm-Related Background Checks Involving Terrorist Watch List Records*, GAO-05-127, January 2005, p. 32.

[48] Statement of Daniel D. Roberts, Assistant Director, Criminal Justice Information Services, Federal Bureau of Investigation, *Terrorists and Guns: The Nature of the Threat and Proposed Reforms: Hearing Before the Senate Committee on Homeland Security and Governmental Affairs*, 111th Cong., May 5, 2010.

[49] U.S. Government Accountability Office, *Terrorist Watchlist Screening: FBI Has Enhanced Its Use of Information from Firearm and Explosives Background Checks to Support Counterterrorism Efforts*, GAO-10-703T, May 2010, p. 8.

[50] Statement of Daniel D. Roberts, Assistant Director, Criminal Justice Information Services, Federal Bureau of Investigation, *Terrorists and Guns: The Nature of the Threat and Proposed Reforms: Hearing Before the Senate Committee on Homeland Security and Governmental Affairs*, 111th Cong., May 5, 2010.

[51] Ibid.

[52] Ibid.

[53] Ibid.

upon the positive encounter and the fact that the watch-listed applicant had attempted to acquire either a firearm or a permit, or an explosives license/permit, if allowable under pertinent Attorney General investigative guidelines.[54] In either case, the TSOU case agent is obligated to respond back to the NICS Command Center within 72 hours so NICS staff will know how to handle the NICS transaction.[55]

After a federally licensed gun dealer receives notice that the transaction may proceed, all identifying information submitted by or on behalf of the transferee is to be destroyed within 24 hours.[56] In the case of a delayed response, all identifying information except for the NTN (NICS Transaction Number) and date of the transaction is to be destroyed in 90 days, unless a prohibiting factor is reported to the NICS Center.[57] Generally, if an FFL proceeds with a transaction at his discretion following three business days, and the applicant is subsequently found to be disqualified, the Bureau of Alcohol, Tobacco, Firearms and Explosives (ATF) is notified and a firearms retrieval action is initiated in coordination with a JTTF.

GAO Report Recommendations (January 2005)

Senators Joseph Biden and Frank Lautenberg requested that GAO report on the modified NICS terrorist watchlist procedures. In January 2005, GAO reported that in a five-month period—February 3, 2004, through June 30, 2004—NICS checks resulted in an estimated 650 terrorist-related record hits.[58] Of these potential hits, 44 were found to be positive matches. Yet, 35 of these transactions were allowed to proceed because, as noted above, being identified as a known or suspected terrorist is not grounds to prohibit a person from being transferred a firearm. Another six were denied, one was unresolved, and two were of an unknown status.[59] GAO recommended that the Attorney General (1) clarify what information generated by the NICS background check process could be shared with counterterrorism officials; and (2) either more frequently monitor background checks conducted by full and partial POC states that result in terrorism-related NICS hits or allow the FBI to handle these cases entirely.[60] Following this GAO recommendation, NICS procedures were altered and the NICS and TSC staff currently handle all KST hits for both full and partial POC states. However, with regard to the former recommendation, it is unknown whether the Attorney General clarified what NICS-generated information could be shared with counterterrorism officials.

Possible Issues Raised by the Modified NICS Procedures

When Congress passed the Brady Act in November 1993, the use of terrorist watchlists during firearms-related background checks was not considered. Correspondingly, the Attorney General has no specific statutory authority to screen prospective gun buyers against terrorist watchlist

---

[54] Ibid.

[55] Ibid.

[56] Retention and Destruction of Records in the System, 28 C.F.R. §25.9(b)(1)(iii).

[57] Ibid. at §25.9(b)(1)(ii).

[58] U.S. Government Accountability Office, *Gun Control and Terrorism: FBI Could Better Manage Firearm-Related Background Checks Involving Terrorist Watch List Records*, GAO-05-127, January 2005, p. 9.

[59] Ibid.

[60] Ibid.

records. Nevertheless, the DOJ and FBI have adopted procedures to do this because being on such a list suggests that there may be an underlying factor that would bar a prospective background check applicant from possessing a firearm. Hence, a possible issue for Congress could be whether terrorist watchlist checks should be incorporated statutorily into the Brady background checks for firearms.

In addition, a proviso attached to the FY2004 DOJ annual appropriation and every year thereafter requires that NICS-generated approved firearms transaction records be destroyed within 24 hours.[61] As described above, the FBI does not maintain those records for more than 24 hours after a federally licensed gun dealer has been notified by NICS that a firearms transaction has been approved. However, when background checks result in either partial or incomplete criminal history records, or a terrorist watchlist (NCIC-KST) hit, the firearms transactions is delayed for up to three business days. If a final determination cannot be made within three business days, NICS staff maintains the transaction record in an "open" status for up to 90 days. Upon a final determination, the FBI destroys the NICS firearms transaction records if the transferee is not found to be a prohibited person. However, to reach this final determination, information on the subjects of those background checks is passed on to FBI Special Agents and Intelligence Analysts in the field. While the NICS records are eventually destroyed for approved firearms transfers, it is unknown what happens to the information generated by NICS-related terrorist watchlist hits that are passed on to the FBI Counterterrorism Division and investigative personnel in the field, who are usually assigned to Joint Terrorism Task Forces. Information about those firearms transactions is possibly recorded and stored electronically in the FBI's investigative case files.

In the Brady Act, moreover, there is a provision that prohibits the (1) transfer of any Brady system record to any other federal or state agency, or (2) the use of the Brady system as a national registry of firearms, firearms owners, or firearms transactions or dispositions.[62] In light of the former prohibition, a second issue for Congress could be whether to grant the FBI greater authority to maintain and access NICS records for the purposes of counterterrorism, or whether existing statutory limitations that were arguably designed to prevent the maintenance of and access to such records should be strengthened.

In light of the first two issues, it follows that a third issue for Congress could be whether the Attorney General should be given explicit authority to deny firearms transfers to watch-listed persons on a case-by-case basis, or whether all known or suspected terrorists should be statutorily prohibited from possessing firearms and explosives.

---

[61] In the Consolidated and Further Continuing Appropriations Act, 2012 (P.L. 112-55), Congress "futurity" language in this provision (§511), which makes the provision permanent law, as opposed to an annual appropriations restriction. This provision was first added to the FY2004 CJS Appropriations bill (H.R. 2799) as part of a larger amendment that Representative Todd Tiahrt offered in full appropriations committee markup. For further information, see CRS Report RS22458, *Gun Control: Statutory Disclosure Limitations on ATF Firearms Trace Data and Multiple Handgun Sales Reports*, by William J. Krouse.

[62] For example, subsection 103(i) of the Brady Act (P.L. 103-159; 107 Stat. 1542) includes the following provision: PROHIBITION RELATING TO ESTABLISHMENT OF REGISTRATION SYSTEMS WITH RESPECT TO FIREARMS. – No department, agency, officer, or employee of the United States may – (1) require that any record or portion thereof generated by the system established under this section be recorded at or transferred to a facility owned, managed, or controlled by the United States or any State or political subdivision thereof; or (2) use the system established under this section to establish any system for the registration of firearms, firearm owners, or firearm transaction or disposition, except with respect to persons, prohibited by section 922 (g) or (n) of title 18, United States Code or State law, from receiving a firearm.

In the 109th Congress, several pieces of legislation were introduced that were related to NICS background checks and terrorist watchlists. For example, Senator Lautenberg and Representative John Conyers introduced the Terrorist Apprehension and Record Retention Act of 2005 (S. 578/H.R. 1225), a bill that would have (1) required that the FBI, along with appropriate federal and state counterterrorism officials, be notified immediately when NICS background checks indicated that a person seeking to obtain a firearm was a known or suspected terrorist; (2) required that the FBI coordinate the response to these occurrences; and (3) authorized the retention of all related records for at least 10 years. In both the 110th and 111th Congresses, Senator Lautenberg introduced a similar proposal, the Preserving Records of Terrorists & Criminals Transactions Act (S. 2935 and S. 2820).

Also, in the 109th Congress Representative Peter King introduced H.R. 1168, a bill that would have required the Attorney General to promulgate regulations to preserve records of terrorist- and gang-related matches during these background checks until they had been provided to the FBI. Although these proposals would have addressed the issue of record retention, they would not have provided the Attorney General with a specific statutory authority to conduct terrorist watchlist checks, nor would they have authorized the Attorney General to deny a firearms transfer based solely on a terrorist watchlist match. However, Representative Carolyn McCarthy introduced a proposal in the 109th Congress (H.R. 1195) that would have barred anyone on the "No Fly" list from possessing a firearm.[63] Prompted by some Members of Congress, DOJ developed a proposal to authorize the Attorney General to deny a firearms transfer to any watch-listed person he deemed to be a "dangerous terrorist," as discussed below.

DOJ Draft Proposal (April 2007)

Although watch-listed persons may be subjects of ongoing foreign intelligence, national security, and criminal investigations, they may not be persons prohibited from possessing firearms or explosives under current federal law. As subsequent events would indicate, DOJ concluded that it was limited under current law in its authority to use terrorist watchlists as part of the background check processes to deny firearms and explosives transfers to known or suspected terrorists. In hearings before the House Committee on the Judiciary, then-Attorney General Alberto Gonzales was questioned several times by Members of Congress about NICS procedures and terrorist watchlist hits.

> Representative Chris Van Hollen: "Does it make sense to you that we stop a person from boarding the airline in order to protect the public safety, [but] that an individual can turn around, get in their car, go to the local gun shop and buy 20 semiautomatic assault weapons?"
>
> Attorney General Gonzales: "I think we should be doing everything we can to ensure that people [who] are in fact terrorists shouldn't have weapons in this country, the truth of the matter is. But unless they are disabled [disqualified] from having a weapon under the statute there's not much that we can do other than maybe try and get them out of the country or, by the way, to see if there's any disability under the statute that would allow us to deny them a firearm."[64]

---

[63] The "No Fly" list is a terrorist watchlist employed by TSA to screen passengers prior to boarding commercial aircraft and other conveyances.

[64] Testimony of Alberto Gonzales, Attorney General, Department of Justice, *USA Patriot Act: A Review for the* (continued...)

In 2005, Attorney General Gonzales directed the DOJ to form a working group to review federal gun laws—particularly in regard to NICS background checks—to examine whether additional authority should be sought to prevent firearms transfers to known or suspected terrorists.[65] Nearly two years later, in April 2007, DOJ proposed legislation that would give the Attorney General the authority to deny a firearms transfer, state-issued firearms permit, or explosive license to any person found "to be or have been engaged in conduct constituting, in preparation for, in aid of, or related to terrorism."[66] In the 110th Congress, Senator Lautenberg and Representative King introduced this proposal (S. 1237/H.R. 2074), but no further action was taken on either bill. In addition, Representative McCarthy reintroduced her proposal, newly titled the No Fly, No Buy Act (H.R. 1167).

GAO Follow-Up Report (May 2009)

In May 2009, nearly four years after its first report on NICS-related terrorist watchlist hits, GAO issued a follow-up report. According to that report, from February 2004 through February 2009 there were

- 963 NICS background checks that resulted in positive terrorist watchlist matches, and of those checks, about 90% (865) were allowed to proceed and a firearms or explosives transfer may have occurred;

- of those checks described above that resulted in positive terrorist watchlist matches and a proceed with transfer, only one involved a potential explosives transfer; and

- of the 10% that resulted in denials (98), the denials were based on felony convictions, illegal immigration status, fugitive from justice status, or the unlawful use of, or addiction to, a controlled substance. All of these denials involved firearms, as opposed to explosives.[67]

GAO also recommended that if Congress were to move forward with legislation providing the Attorney General with the discretionary authority to deny a firearms transfer or permit or an explosives license/permit based on a terrorist watchlist hit, then it should consider including a provision in that legislation that would require the Attorney General to promulgate guidelines that would delineate under what circumstances that authority could be exercised. Following this report, Representative King and Senator Lautenberg reintroduced the DOJ draft proposal as

---

(...continued)

Purpose of Reauthorization: Hearing Before H. Comm. on the Judiciary, 109th Cong. 81-82, April 6, 2005.

[65] See U.S. Department of Justice, Office of Legislative Affairs, Letter to the Honorable Richard B. Cheney, President, United States Senate, from Richard A. Hertling Acting Assistant Attorney General, February 13, 2007, http://lautenberg.senate.gov/assets/terrorgap/Feb_2007_DOJ_Reply.pdf; Letter to Honorable Robert S. Mueller, III, Director of the Federal Bureau of Investigation and Honorable Alberto Gonzales, Attorney General, November 1, 2006, http://lautenberg.senate.gov/assets/terrorgap/2006_Lautenberg_Biden_Letter.pdf.

[66] This proposal was drafted by the Department of Justice for consideration by Congress. See U.S. Department of Justice, Office of Legislative Affairs, Letter to the Honorable Richard B. Cheney, President, United States Senate, from Richard A. Hertling Acting Assistant Attorney General, April 25, 2007, http://lautenberg.senate.gov/assets/terrorgap/Cheney_DOJ_Drafted_Bill_Re_Dangerous_Terrorists_Act_2007.pdf.

[67] U.S. Government Accountability Office, , *Firearm and Explosive Background Checks Involving Terrorist Watch List Records*, GAO-09-125R, May 2009, p. 8.

nearly identical bills (H.R. 2159 and S. 1317), which supporters dubbed the "Terror Gap" proposal.[68]

Terror Gap Legislation

During the 111th Congress, the November 5, 2009, Fort Hood shooting, in which 13 persons were shot to death and 32 wounded, served to heighten congressional interest in the use of terrorist screening records and firearms-related background checks. Leading up to the shooting, the alleged shooter, U.S. Army Major Nidal Malik Hasan, had corresponded by email with a radical Muslim imam, Anwar al-Aulaqi, who U.S. authorities had long suspected of having substantial ties to al-Qaeda in the Arabian Peninsula.[69] Although FBI counterterrorism agents had been aware of Hasan's communications with al-Aulaqi,[70] it was unclear at what level Hasan was scrutinized by the FBI.[71] If he had been the subject of a full counterterrorism investigation, FBI policy would have required that he be watch-listed as a known or suspected terrorist.[72] Had Hasan been watch-listed, there is a possibility, depending on the sequence of events, that his purchase of a pistol and the required Brady background check could have alerted FBI counterterrorism agents to that transfer, and they might have been able to take steps that would have prevented the shooting.[73] This event and several other terrorist attacks or disrupted plots involving firearms prompted Members of Congress to reexamine the Terror Gap proposal.

HSGAC Hearing on the Fort Hood Shooting

In May 2010, HSGAC held a hearing on "terrorists and guns," during which issues related to the Fort Hood shooting and a proposal to give the Attorney General additional authority to deny firearms transactions to persons watch-listed as terrorists were explored.[74] Senator Joseph

---

[68] Also, in the 111th Congress Representative McCarthy reintroduced the No Fly, No Buy Act (H.R. 2401). And, Senator Lautenberg introduced a bill that would have allowed the Attorney General to maintain NICS records on approved transfers that were also related terrorist watchlist hits (S. 2820). Congressional attention following the Fort Hood shooting, however, was largely focused on the Terror Gap proposal.

[69] Carrie Johnson, Spencer C. Hsu, and Ellen Nakashima, "Hasan Had Intensified Contact with Cleric: FBI Monitored E-mail Exchanges Fort Hood Suspect Raised Prospect of Financial Transfers," *Washington Post*, November 21, 2009, p. A01.

[70] Philip Rucker, Carrie Johnson, and Ellen Nakashima, "Hasan E-mails to Cleric Didn't Result in Inquiry; Suspect in Fort Hood Shootings Will Be Tried in Military Court," *Washington Post*, November 10, 2009, p. A01.

[71] According to a November 11, 2009, FBI press release, Hasan's communications with Anwar al-Aulaqi were assessed by the FBI in connection with an investigation of another subject, and the content of those communications was explainable by his research as a psychiatrist at the Walter Reed Medical Center and nothing else derogatory was found that would have suggested that he was involved in terrorist activities or planning; U.S. Department of Justice, Federal Bureau of Investigation, *Investigation Continues Into Fort Hood Shooting*, November 11, 2009, http://www.fbi.gov/news/pressrel/press-releases/investigation-continues-into-fort-hood-shooting.

[72] U.S. Department of Justice, Office of the Inspector General, Audit Division, *Federal Bureau of Investigation's Terrorist Watchlist Nomination Practices*, Report 09-25, May 2009, p. 11.

[73] Michael Bloomberg and Thomas Kean, "Enabling the Next Fort Hood? Congress's Curbs on Gun Data Hurt Investigations," *Washington Post*, November 27, 2009, p. A23.

[74] *Terrorists and Guns: The Nature of the Threat and Proposed Reforms: Hearing Before the Senate Committee on Homeland Security and Governmental Affairs*, 111th Cong. May 5, 2010, CQ Congressional Transcripts. For further information on Muslim extremists and terrorist plots in the United States, see CRS Report R41416, *American Jihadist Terrorism: Combating a Complex Threat*, by Jerome P. Bjelopera.

Lieberman, chairman of HSGAC, noted that firearms had been used in at least two deadly terrorist plots perpetrated by "radicalized jihadists": the Fort Hood shooting and the June 2009 Little Rock, AR, recruiting center shooting in which two U.S. servicemen were shot—one killed and one wounded. In other thwarted plots, conspirators were arrested for planning to use firearms to attack servicemen at Fort Dix, NJ, in 2006 and the Quantico, VA, Marine base in 2009.[75] As part of his opening statement, Senator Lieberman voiced his strong support for the Terror Gap legislation and urged its prompt passage.[76] He observed that

> Terrorists armed with semi-automatic and high-powered weapons can inflict heavy casualties in seconds. While it is true that homegrown terrorists are generally less sophisticated than those sponsored and trained overseas by Al Qaeda, they may also – particularly if acting alone – be harder to detect and stop. And the easy availability of lethal weapons ensures that these homegrown terrorists can legally obtain sufficient firepower to cause terrible damage.[77]

These concerns were reinforced in June 2011 when Al Qaeda's U.S.-born spokesperson, Adam Gadahn, exhorted Muslim extremists in the United States to acquire firearms and carry out terrorist attacks in the United States in an internet posting.[78]

For the hearing, GAO released updated statistics on firearms and explosives background checks and subsequent transactions that involved individuals watch-listed as terrorists.[79] GAO also reported on measures taken by the FBI to improve firearms and explosives background checks for counterterrorism purposes. In this update, GAO reiterated that if Congress were to move forward with legislation providing the Attorney General with the discretionary authority to deny firearms or explosives transfers to individuals watch-listed as terrorists, then it should consider including a provision in that legislation to require the Attorney General to promulgate guidelines that would delineate under what circumstances such authority could be exercised.[80]

Daniel Roberts, FBI Assistant Director for the Criminal Justice Information Services Division, also testified about the modified background procedures that were adopted in February 2004 to include terrorist watchlist screening as part of firearms and explosives background checks.[81] In

---

[75] Ibid.

[76] Opening Statement of Chairman Joseph I. Lieberman, Senate Committee on Homeland Security and Governmental Affairs, *Terrorists and Guns: The Nature of the Threat and Proposed Reforms*, May 5, 2010, available at http://hsgac.senate.gov/public/index.cfm?FuseAction=Hearings.Hearing&Hearing_ID=a6061b56-3636-4fac-8446-b3c0dd65d02d.

[77] Ibid.

[78] Larry McShane, "Terror At Gun Store. U.S. Great Place To Buy Firearms, 'American Al Qaeda' Tells Jihadis," *Daily News* (New York), June 4, 2011, p. 6.

[79] U.S. Government Accountability Office, *Terrorist Watchlist Screening: FBI Has Enhanced Its Use of Information from Firearm and Explosives Background Checks to Support Counterterrorism Efforts*, GAO-10-703T, May 2010. In this report, GAO reported that from February 2004 through February 2010, there were 1,228 positive encounters through NICS-related firearms or explosives transactions with individuals who had been placed on a terrorist watchlist. These encounters involved 650 individuals because 450 of these individuals were involved in multiple transactions. Six of these individuals were involved in 10 or more transactions. In 1,119 encounters, the transactions were allowed to proceed. In 109 encounters, the transactions were denied. From March 2009 to February 2010, there were 272 positive encounters and all of the transactions were allowed to proceed, including one that involved explosives.

[80] As described below, such a provision has been included in the Senate version of the Terror Gap proposal (S. 34), but it has not been included in the House version (H.R. 1506).

[81] Statement of Daniel D. Roberts, Assistant Director, Criminal Justice Information Services, Federal Bureau of Investigation, *Terrorists and Guns: The Nature of the Threat and Proposed Reforms: Hearing Before the Senate Committee on Homeland Security and Governmental Affairs*, 111th Cong., May 5, 2010.

addition, GAO reported that in October 2008, the FBI Counterterrorism Division initiated an analysis of firearms and explosives background checks that resulted in terrorist watchlist hits as a precaution prior to the presidential inauguration.[82] Based on this analysis, the Counterterrorism Division began issuing analytical reports on this data on a monthly and quarterly basis.[83] These classified reports are circulated to FBI field offices and Joint Terrorism Task Forces (JTTFs), and they have reportedly been instrumental in several FBI investigations.[84] FBI officials indicated to GAO that they are generally allowed to collect, retain, and share information on watch-listed individuals who have engaged in a firearms or explosives transaction, regardless of whether the transaction was denied or allowed to proceed.[85] Hence, background checks for firearms and explosives have arguably become a valuable source of criminal intelligence for the FBI.

Senator Lautenberg and Representative King testified in support of their bills (S. 1317 and H.R. 2159). Both New York City Mayor Michael R. Bloomberg and Police Chief Raymond W. Kelly also testified in favor of these bills. Los Angeles Assistant Police Chief Sandy Jo MacArthur testified about the Los Angeles Police Department's ability to respond to events involving multiple attacks with firearms and/or explosives. Underscoring that many criminal assailants and terrorists often choose long guns and explosives, MacArthur opined that the "tools" (statutes) used to prevent firearms from falling into the hands of felons and domestic violence misdemeanants ought to be applied to known or suspected terrorists.[86]

Conversely, Liberty Coalition Privacy Director Aaron Titus avowed that the Terror Gap legislation would "strip citizens of their enumerated constitutional right to bear arms without any meaningful due process."[87] Senator Lindsey Graham concurred, arguing that denying a firearms transfer based on a felony conviction in a lawful court was fundamentally different from doing so based on a terrorist watchlist record. He emphasized that watchlist records are created by an investigator or intelligence analyst based upon his reasonable suspicion that the subject is a terrorist or terrorist supporter. Given that firearms possession for self defense is protected as an individual right under the Second Amendment of the Constitution, he surmised that such a denial would be improper.[88] Similarly, Senator Susan Collins observed that denying a firearms transfer raises issues, possibly constitutional in nature, that denying an explosives license or permit would not.[89]

Denying Firearms and Explosives to Dangerous Terrorists Act of 2011 (S. 34 and H.R. 1506)

In a February 2011 special report, the HSGAC categorized the November 2009 Fort Hood shooting as the worst terrorist attack on U.S. soil since the 9/11 attacks.[90] Senator Lautenberg and

---

[82] Ibid. at 9.

[83] Ibid.

[84] Ibid.

[85] Ibid. at 10.

[86] *Terrorists and Guns: The Nature of the Threat and Proposed Reforms: Hearing Before the Senate Committee on Homeland Security and Governmental Affairs*, 111th Cong. May 5, 2010, CQ Congressional Transcripts.

[87] Ibid.

[88] Ibid.

[89] Ibid.

[90] U.S. Senate Committee on Homeland Security and Governmental Affairs, *A Ticking Time Bomb: Counterterrorism* (continued...)

Representative King reintroduced their Terror Gap proposal as the Denying Firearms and Explosives to Dangerous Terrorists Act of 2011 (S. 34 and H.R. 1506). Supporters include 550 mayors of U.S. cities, who are represented by Mayors Against Illegal Guns.[91] They assert that if the federal government can stop an individual on a terrorist watchlist from boarding a commercial aircraft, then the federal government ought to be empowered to stop an individual on a terrorist watchlist from acquiring a firearm. Opponents of the bill, including the National Rifle Association (NRA), argue that the Terror Gap proposal, if enacted, would be unconstitutional because it would allow the Attorney General to deny a person his "individual right to keep and bear arms," and do so "without due process of law."[92] Supporters of the Terror Gap bill counter that it would provide a level of redress and remedy that are currently unavailable to others who face a denial of some other benefit or activity because they are identified as known or suspected terrorists through other federal terrorist screening activities.

Firearms Eligibility and Dangerous Terrorist Determination

The Terror Gap bill would grant the Attorney General discretionary authority to make a determination and designate an individual as a "dangerous terrorist." This determination would be the basis for a denial of a firearms transfer, state-issued firearms permit, or an explosives or firearms-related federal firearms license. Brady background checks would likely trigger this determination because the bill would amend provisions of current law related to firearms and explosives eligibility and to background checks conducted through NICS. The Attorney General could make the determination if the individual in question

> is known (or appropriately suspected) to be or have been engaged in conduct constituting, preparation for, in aid of, or related to terrorism, or providing material support or resources for terrorism, and [there is] a reasonable belief that the [individual] may use a firearm in connection with terrorism.[93]

This provision could have been designed to be discretionary for several possible reasons. First, not all individuals who are watch-listed as known or suspected terrorists present the same potential level or type of threat to public safety and/or national security. Second, there are likely individuals whom federal intelligence officers and counterterrorism agents would want to monitor more closely if given the option, but they would not want to alert those individuals to the possibility that they had been identified and watch-listed as a known or suspected terrorist. Indeed, there may be occasions when FBI counterterrorism agents would want to allow a firearms transfer to proceed so that they could surveil the known or suspected terrorist to see what he might do with that firearm or see to whom he might subsequently transfer those firearms. Third,

---

(...continued)
Lessons from the U.S. Government's Failure to Prevent the Fort Hood Attack, A Special Report by Joseph I. Lieberman, Chairman, and Susan M. Collins, Ranking Member, February 3, 2011, p. 7.

[91] Letter from Mayors Against Illegal Guns to the Honorable John Boehner, Speaker of the House, and the Honorable Harry Reid, Senate Majority Leader, *Re: 550 Mayors Call on Congress to Support H.R. 1506/S. 34 and Close the "Terror Gap,"* May 11, 2011.

[92] National Rifle Association, Institute for Legislative Action, "Keeping An Eye On 'Terror Watchlist' Legislation," May 20, 2011.

[93] Proposed 18 U.S.C. §§922A and B. The proposal would define "terrorism" as both international and domestic terrorism as defined at 18 U.S.C. §2331, and define "material support or resources" as defined at 18 U.S.C. §2339A. For further information on material support, see CRS Report R41333, *Terrorist Material Support: An Overview of 18 U.S.C. 2339A and 2339B*, by Charles Doyle.

the Attorney General may not want to call undue public attention to terrorist screening sources and methods that a denied, high-profile firearm(s) transfer might generate if and when a "dangerous terrorist" determination were made public.

On the other hand, the bill could be viewed as making the Attorney General responsible for making risk assessments about all potential firearms transfers that involved terrorist watchlist hits, despite the discretionary nature of the provision. While these risk assessments are already being performed at some level under the modified firearms background check procedures, this new authority, once granted, could create a public expectation that the Attorney General and his subordinates would always be correct in making the risk assessments. Consequently, if a watch-listed person were allowed to acquire a firearm from a federally licensed gun dealer, perhaps mistakenly, and he went on to commit a terrorist act, particularly one involving a mass shooting and loss of life, many in the public may perceive the Attorney General as being responsible for that outcome.

Notification of a Dangerous Terrorist Determination

Under the bill, the Attorney General would also be granted discretion about whether to inform a watch-listed and denied individual of the underlying "dangerous terrorist" determination that had been made about him. Hence, the Attorney General could potentially follow several paths with regard to any watch-listed person:

- decline to make the determination and allow the transfer to go forward;
- make the determination, notify the individual, and deny the transfer; or
- make the determination, decline to notify the individual, but deny the transfer.

Under current law, however, an individual who is prohibited from being transferred a firearm has a right to learn the reason(s) for his firearms transfer denial. Whether notified or not, a person denied a firearms transfer under the bill would presumably be able to follow the same procedures in an attempt to learn the reason(s) for his denial. Under the bill, if the FBI continued the policy of neither confirming nor denying whether a person was watch-listed and was therefore unable to inform the individual about the reason for his denial, the individual might deduce that he had been watch-listed, because he would have been informed for any other reason(s).

Tenth Class of Prohibited Persons Under 18 U.S.C. §922(g)

The bill would add persons whom the Attorney General had given "actual notice" of a "dangerous terrorist" determination to the nine classes of persons who are already prohibited from shipping, transporting, possessing, or receiving a firearm or ammunition under the GCA.[94] As a result, any firearms previously possessed by the individual would become illegal upon notification of a "dangerous terrorist" determination. He would be obliged to give up control over any firearms he possessed until he successfully challenged the Attorney General's determination in federal court (as described below). On the other hand, if the Attorney General should choose not to notify the individual about the "dangerous terrorist" determination, the denied individual would continue to be legally eligible to possess any firearms that he previously possessed, as long as his previous

---

[94] 18 U.S.C. §922(g).

possession were legal. It would also be legal for him to acquire firearms from private persons if those transfers were intrastate and in compliance with state laws. The bill would also prohibit any person from knowingly transferring a firearm to *any* person determined to be a "dangerous terrorist" by the Attorney General, although it is unclear how anyone in the general public (i.e., private persons) would be aware of that determination.

Remedies for Erroneous Firearms Denials

With regard to NICS denials and "dangerous terrorist" determinations, the bill would amend the Brady Act to allow a denied individual to request from the Attorney General notification of the reason(s) for the denial, but it would also give the Attorney General the authority to withhold those reasons if he determines that the disclosure would compromise national security.[95] The bill would make a similar amendment to the Brady Act in regard to correcting erroneous information.[96] Any denied person would also be able to challenge that determination in U.S. federal court within 60 days of notice. The court would be required to sustain the Attorney General's determination upon a showing by the U.S. government by a preponderance of the evidence standard that the determination satisfied the proposed provisions described above (18 U.S.C. §§922A and B).

Pursuing remedy under the bill could prove very difficult because it would give the Attorney General considerable latitude to withhold from the court any information that would compromise national security. The court would be allowed access to summaries or redacted versions of documents underlying those determinations, as long as those documents did not contain information that might compromise national security. The bill does not address, however, whether the petitioner (denied person) or his attorney would be allowed access to those documents. In addition, at the court's option or on the motion of the petitioner, the court would be allowed to review the full, undisclosed documents *ex parte* and *in camera*.[97] The court would also be allowed to determine whether the summaries or redacted versions of those documents were fair and accurate representations of the underlying documents. However, the court would not be allowed to overturn the Attorney General's determination based solely on the full, undisclosed documents.

Furthermore, the bill does not address any of the implications of a determination being overturned. For example, if the petitioner were erroneously placed on the list, would there be any obligation on the part of the Attorney General to remove him from the watchlist? Or, if the petitioner were misidentified as a known or suspected terrorist, would some other form of redress be appropriate? One possible remedy under the bill could be a court order directing the firearms transfer, although this is unclear. Notwithstanding these ambiguities, the "remedies" provisions of the bill could possibly serve as a precedent under which other individuals adversely affected by the use of terrorist watchlists could challenge the outcomes of other terrorist screening activities conducted by frontline screening agencies in federal court. As described above, individuals who believe they have been misidentified as a terrorist while being screened by TSA or CBP, or other frontline screening agencies, arguably have narrower avenues for relief than that which would be provided under the bill.

---

[95] P.L. 103-159, Section 103(f); 107 Stat. 1542 (1993).

[96] P.L. 103-159, Section 103(g); 107 Stat. 1542. (1993).

[97] *Ex parte* means a proceeding in which the defendant is not present or represented. *In camera* means either the hearing is before the judge in his chambers or all spectators and jurors are excluded from the courtroom.

Denial and Revocation of Firearms and Explosives Licenses

The bill would also make similar amendments to firearms and explosives licensing statutes.[98] Accordingly, as it does for firearms, the bill would prohibit any individual who had received notice of a determination by the Attorney General that he was a "dangerous terrorist" from shipping, transporting, possessing, or receiving any explosive. In addition, the Attorney General would have the authority under the bill to deny or revoke any federal firearms license or explosives license or permit if he determines that the prospective or current holder of a firearms license or an explosives license or permit[99] is a known or suspected terrorist, and there is a reasonable belief that he might use firearms or explosives in a terrorist act. Interestingly, the bill does not address the renewal of such licenses or permits. Hence, the bill could be interpreted as authorizing the Attorney General to screen licensees and permit holders on a continuous basis to determine whether they have been watch-listed as known or suspected terrorists and then consider whether these persons should be determined to be "dangerous terrorists." Although the bill would allow an individual to challenge the denial or revocation of either a firearms license or explosives license/permit in federal court, it would similarly authorize the Attorney General to withhold certain information in those lawsuits if its disclosure could compromise national security.

Attorney General Implementing Guidelines

Although S. 34 and H.R. 1506 are nearly identical, the Senate bill includes an additional provision. As recommended by GAO in 2009, it would require the Attorney General to issue guidelines outlining the circumstances under which the authority to make "dangerous terrorist" determinations would be exercised. The guidelines would be intended to provide accountability and a basis for monitoring how the authority is exercised so that the intended goals and expected results of the bill are achieved. This would arguably be done in a manner that safeguards privacy and civil liberties in accordance with Homeland Security Presidential Directives, under which the George W. Bush Administration sought to strengthen terrorist screening policies and procedures.

Possible Policy Issues Raised by the Terror Gap Proposal

Arguments for the Terror Gap bill and similar proposals often coalesce around the need for greater public safety in light of the fact that terrorists have used, or plotted to use, firearms and explosives in attacks in the United States. Conversely, arguments against the Terror Gap bill could coalesce around several issues, including the feasibility of non-notification, adequate opportunity for redress, and possible precedents for judicial review.

---

[98] 18 U.S.C. §§841 *et seq.*; Organized Crime Control Act, P.L. 91-452; 84 Stat. 952 (1970).

[99] Under federal explosives law, permits are issued to responsible persons. A "responsible person" is defined in 18 U.S.C. §841(s) as "an individual who has the power to direct the management policies of the applicant pertaining to explosive materials." In other words, these permits are issued to employees of explosives licensees who have access to and handle explosives. Under federal firearms law, there is no similar analog with regard to employees of federally licensed guns dealers.

Would the Proposed Non-notification Authority Be Feasible?

Under the Terror Gap bill, the Attorney General would have the discretionary authority to deny a firearms transfer to any person that he determined to be a "dangerous terrorist," but he would also have the authority to choose whether to notify the subject of that determination. As previously discussed, under the Brady Act, however, the agency holding the prohibiting record(s) on an individual is obligated to inform a denied person of the reason(s) for his NICS denial.[100] On the other hand, it is generally the policy of the federal government to neither confirm nor deny whether an individual has been placed on a terrorist watchlist. If not notified of the "dangerous terrorist" determination, the denied person could inquire about the reason for the denial. If no reason were given for the denial upon inquiry, the denied person might deduce that he had been placed on a terrorist watchlist; otherwise, he would have been informed of the reason for denial. Some observers might question whether the policy of neither confirming nor denying whether an individual is watch-listed following a firearms denial based on a "dangerous terrorist" determination would be sustainable in the long run. In other words, if the only possible deduction that a denied person could make is that he was on a terrorist watchlist, why not tell him so?

Would Adequate Opportunity for Redress and Remedy Be Provided?

Denied individuals who believe they have been misidentified or mistakenly placed on a terrorist watchlist could face formidable obstacles to seeking redress. Proponents of the Terror Gap bill could argue that the FBI would most likely respond to the denied person within five business days, leaving them 60 days to conclude that they had been placed on a terrorist watchlist in the case of non-notification, and then hire an attorney and present their case in a federal court. Opponents of the proposal could counter that a person mistakenly determined to be a "dangerous terrorist" would have little opportunity to make an effective legal challenge to clear his name, particularly if he were not explicitly notified by the Attorney General of the determination. Furthermore, opponents could argue that, due to the extraordinary nature of a "dangerous terrorist" determination, a petitioner should be afforded more time to mount a legal challenge. A possible issue for Congress could be whether a petitioner would have sufficient time under the bill to appeal a denial in federal court, especially in a case where the Attorney General chose not to inform him of a "dangerous terrorist" determination.

Would a Precedent Be Set for Other Screening Processes?

Supporters of the Terror Gap proposal have argued that it would provide a denied person an opportunity to appeal a "dangerous terrorist" determination that is currently unavailable to individuals identified as known or suspected terrorists in other federal government screening operations, such as passenger screening at an airport. At the same time, opponents of the proposal could argue that such redress and remedy provisions, if implemented, would likely draw unwanted attention to the U.S. government's use of terrorist watchlists and set a precedent for providing judicial review to persons who are adversely affected by the federal government's use of terrorist watchlists and screening operations.

---

[100] Correction of Erroneous System Information, 28 C.F.R. §25.10.

Appendix. Acronyms and Abbreviations

ATF: Alcohol, Tobacco, Firearms and Explosives

CA: Bureau of Consular Affairs

CTD: Counterterrorism Division

CBP: Customs and Border Protection

DHS: Department of Homeland Security

DOJ: Department of Justice

DOS: Department of State

FBI: Federal Bureau of Investigation

FFL: Federal Firearms Licensee

GAO: Government Accountability Office

GCA: Gun Control Act

HSPD-6: Homeland Security Presidential Directive Six

IC: Intelligence Community

JTTF: Joint Terrorism Task Force

KST File: Known or Suspected Terrorists File

NCIC: National Crime Information Center

NCTC: National Counterterrorism Center

NICS: National Instant Criminal Background Check System

NTN: NICS Transaction Number

POC: Point-of-contact

TIDE: Terrorist Identities Datamart Environment

TRIP: Traveler Redress and Inquiry Program

TSA: Transportation Security Administration

TSC: Terrorist Screening Center

TSDB: Terrorist Screening Database

TSOU: Terrorist Screening Operations Unit

VAF: NICS Voluntary Appeals File

VGTOF: Violent Gang and Terrorist Organization File

Author Contact Information

William J. Krouse
Specialist in Domestic Security and Crime Policy
wkrouse@crs.loc.gov, 7-2225

Acknowledgments

Vivian S. Chu, Legislative Attorney, contributed to this report.

www.ingramcontent.com/pod-product-compliance
Lightning Source LLC
Chambersburg PA
CBHW081418170526
45166CB00010B/3393